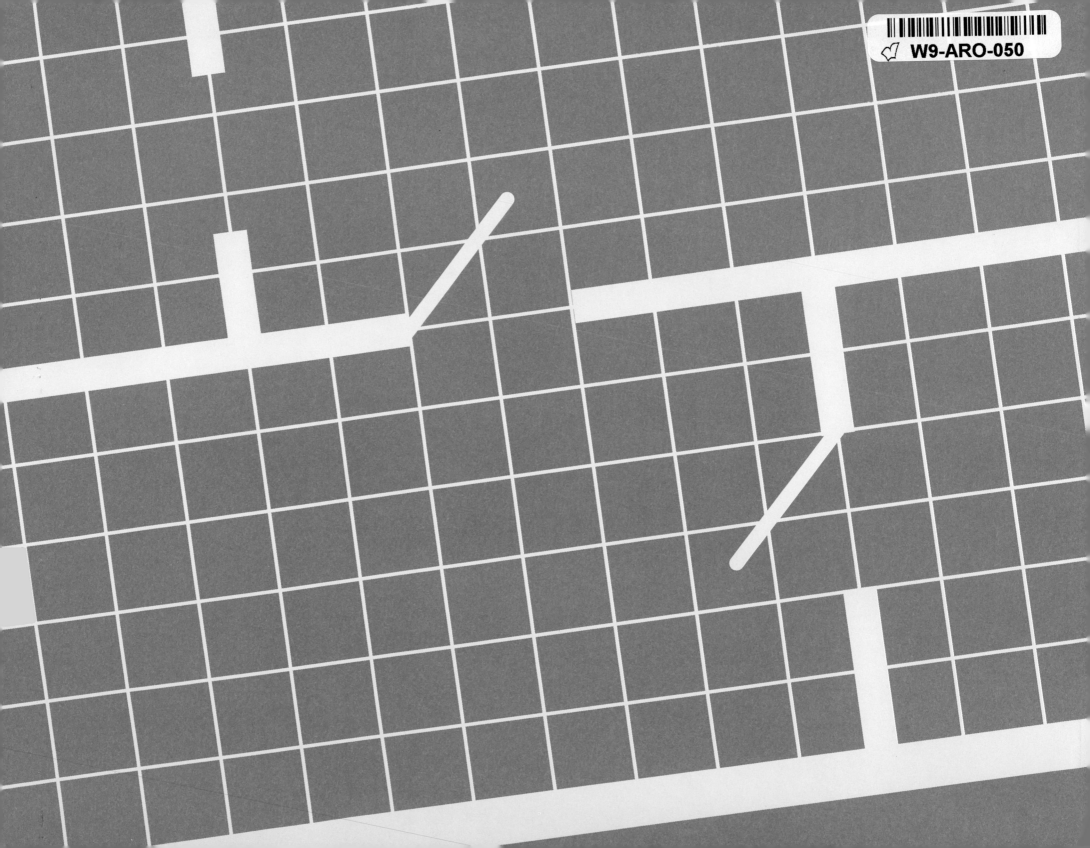

AIRPORT

John Malam

— CONTENTS —

The fold-out section at the start of this book shows the airport terminal building from the outside. Open it up to reveal a cutaway view of the inside, with a key to what happens in each area. After this you will find a plan of the airport complex.

PETER BEDRICK BOOKS

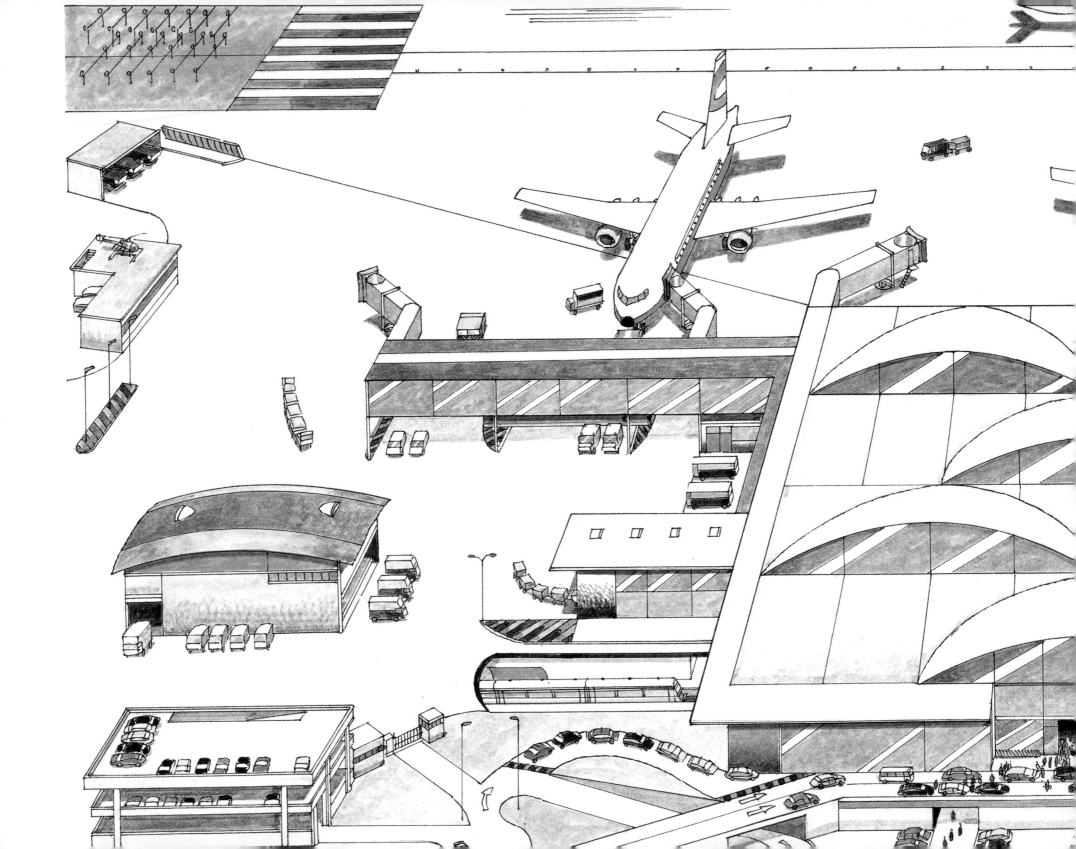

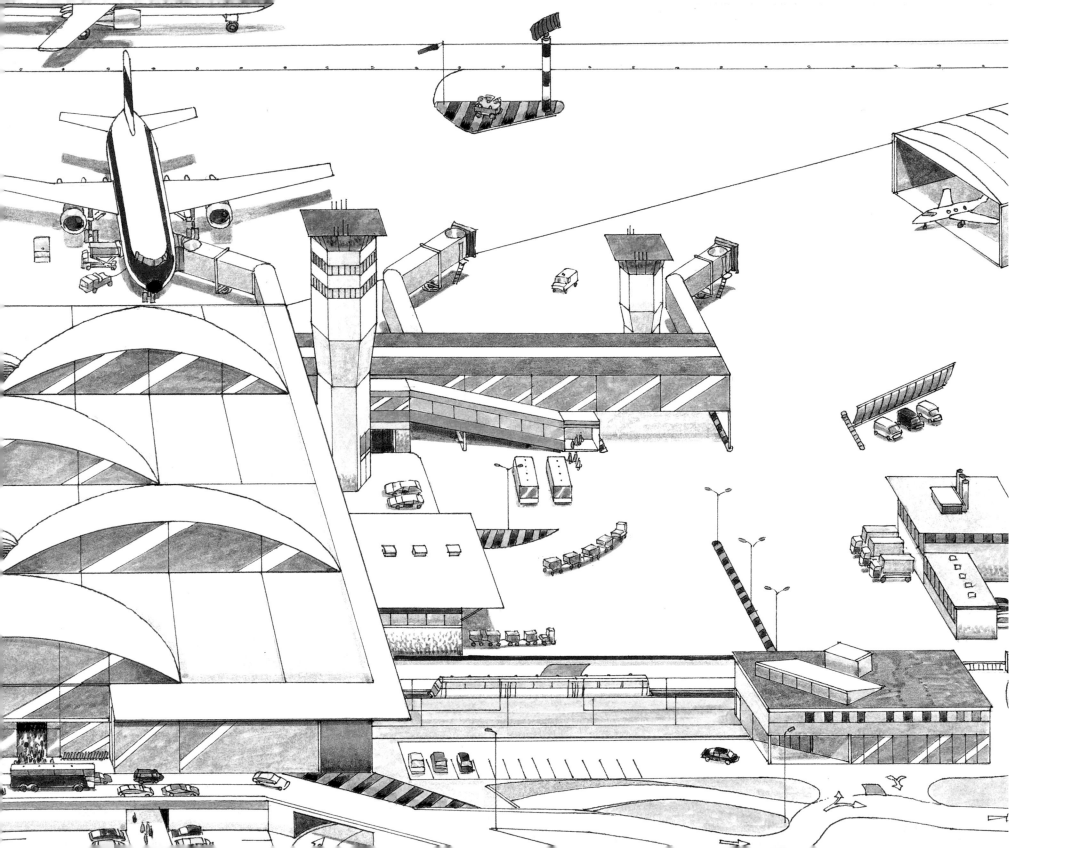

What is an airport?

Millions of travelers pass through an international airport every year, flying to and from destinations all around the world. Thousands of people work here too, every day of the year, often out of sight of the public.

An airport is much more than just a place to catch a plane. Today more people travel by air than ever before, and airports have grown enormously in size. Many of them are like small towns, with shops, offices, banks, parking lots, train stations, fire stations, police and hotels. Many of the facilities are open 24 hours a day. Even in bad weather, when planes cannot use the runways, business goes on as usual elsewhere in the airport.

Many different groups are involved in the planning of a new airport. Architects, designers, town councils and environmental groups work together to create a place that is safe for planes and people. Passengers and freight must be able to reach the airport quickly and easily.

Once it has opened, the airport becomes a workplace for baggage handlers, security staff, airline personnel, air traffic controllers, customs officials, firefighters, caterers, cleaners … and even bird scarers. Lots of other people work behind the scenes. Their work is just as essential to the smooth running of the airport.

This book looks at how a modern international airport works—the type of airport found in major cities all over the world.

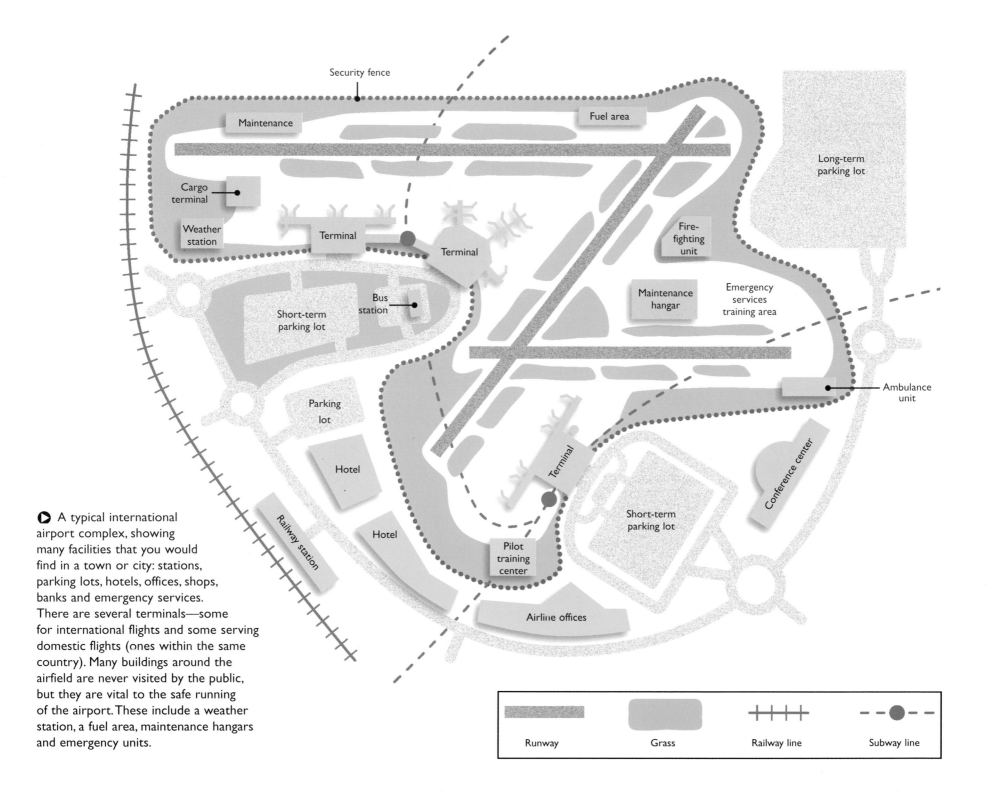

Security fence

Maintenance

Fuel area

Long-term parking lot

Cargo terminal

Weather station

Terminal

Terminal

Fire-fighting unit

Bus station

Maintenance hangar

Emergency services training area

Short-term parking lot

Ambulance unit

Parking lot

Hotel

Railway station

Hotel

Pilot training center

Terminal

Short-term parking lot

Conference center

Airline offices

● A typical international airport complex, showing many facilities that you would find in a town or city: stations, parking lots, hotels, offices, shops, banks and emergency services. There are several terminals—some for international flights and some serving domestic flights (ones within the same country). Many buildings around the airfield are never visited by the public, but they are vital to the safe running of the airport. These include a weather station, a fuel area, maintenance hangars and emergency units.

| Runway | Grass | Railway line | Subway line |

To and from the airport

Most major airports are located well away from built-up areas. This is not only for safety, but also because they need large areas of open, flat land for runways, weather stations, hangars and terminals.

Security officer

Escalator from the subway station.

◀ Subway trains provide a fast link between the airport and nearby towns.

Luggage carts

Airports are well connected to local road and rail networks, so that people and vehicles can reach them quickly and easily.

Main roads lead straight to the airport, bringing people by car, bus and taxi. Passengers going on flights within the same country head for the domestic terminal. Those flying overseas make their way to the international terminal. Trucks carrying cargo follow directions to the freight terminal.

Taxis, and some cars, stop at a drop-off point in front of the departure terminal. They stay just long enough to unload passengers and their bags. Most cars go to short-term parking lots, where parking is limited to a few hours. Some go to long-term parking lots, where they can be left for days or weeks.

Many passengers arrive by train. Buses shuttle back and forth between the station and the airport terminals. In some airports the station is close enough for passengers to take moving walkways.

Some airports are linked to an underground rail network, or subway. The subway station is often built into the airport terminal, from where it is only a short walk to the check-in desks.

Taxis stop briefly at the drop-off point outside the departure terminal.

Check-in

About two hours before passengers are due to fly out from the airport, they make their way to the check-in desks inside the departure terminal.

The departure terminal is a large building, like a huge open hall. Passengers head for the check-in desks with their luggage carts. Large airports may have more than 100 desks, placed together in long lines. Each desk displays the name of the airline company and the flight destination.

Passengers hand over their luggage to be weighed by the airline steward. There are strict limits on the weight of luggage the plane can carry in its hold. If a single item weighs more than 45 pounds, the passenger has to pay an excess baggage charge or leave something behind.

A label is attached to every piece of luggage, enabling it to be tracked around the world. A barcode on the label identifies the flight the case is to be loaded on to by the baggage handlers.

Passengers can keep a small amount of luggage with them, known as carry-on bags. It travels with them in the plane's cabin, usually stored in overhead bins.

An electronic display shows the weight of each case.

Luggage is weighed on this platform.

▶ Passengers check flight information screens to find out where and when to board a flight.

A conveyor belt moves luggage into the baggage handling area.

Barcode label

During check-in, passengers are asked security questions, such as "Did you pack your bags yourself?" and "Have your bags been with you since you packed them?" The questions are designed to find out whether a suspicious item could have been put in the luggage without the owner's knowledge.

Passengers have their flight tickets and passports checked, and are given a boarding pass. This shows their flight details and seat numbers. Without one a passenger cannot pass through the security check point or board a plane.

Going airside

After check-in, passengers can browse around the shops on the "landside" of the airport, which is a public area where people come and go as they please, or they can go "airside."

Only certain people can go airside—passengers with boarding passes and authorized members of the staff. They have to pass through a security check, because this is a restricted area.

Passengers' boarding passes are inspected, and their carry-on bags are passed through an x-ray scanner. The contents of the bags are shown in color on a screen. If security staff see something suspicious on the x-ray, they ask the owner to open the bag for inspection.

Every year thousands of items are confiscated at a busy airport—including party-poppers and small fireworks, which are classed as explosives. Anyone attempting to travel with illegal items is taken to the police.

X-ray machine

Metal detector frame

Hand-held metal detector

▶ A passport is a person's identity document. It allows them to leave one country and enter another.

A color x-ray of a case. Electrical and electronic items appear blue. Plastics appear green. Organic material, such as clothing or paper, looks orange and brown.

Passengers walk through a metal detector frame. If the machine senses a metal object somewhere on, or inside, the person's body, an alarm goes off. The passenger is searched by a security officer. The machine detects keys, coins, jewelery, and hospital pins and plates fixed to bones. All of these are safe to take on to the plane. Objects such as knives and guns are confiscated on the spot, and the passenger is taken away for questioning.

Security is all-important at an airport. Police patrol the buildings, watching for anyone or anything suspicious.

Government officials, presidents, monarchs and celebrities regularly use airports. They, too, must go through the security check before boarding. Until their flight departs, they are protected by the airport police.

Some electrical items, such as this cassette player, are checked very closely for hidden objects. They are also plugged in to see if they work properly.

Departure lounge

Passengers who have been cleared through the security area make their way to the departure lounge. Thousands of people use this area every day while waiting to board their flights.

Some passengers stay in the lounge for only a few minutes. Others may be delayed by several hours, so there are soft seats everywhere, and places to buy snacks, newspapers, magazines and books. More expensive shops sell perfumes, alcohol, chocolates and cameras. There may also be a play area for children.

Monitors display information about flight departures and arrivals.

◀ Business travelers may go into a room next to the departure lounge. Here they can use desks, fax machines, computers and telephones.

▶ A passenger cannot get on to a plane without a boarding pass.

Announcements over the public address system tell people when it is time to board their plane. The same information appears on screens all around the lounge, showing which departure gate to report to.

Passengers not already waiting at the gate make their way down a long corridor called a pier, which is built out over the edge of the airfield. Along the pier are doors, known as gates, which link the building with the planes parked outside.

At the departure gate passengers show their boarding passes to an airline official, who checks they are getting on to the correct plane. There is usually a short wait at the gate until the plane is ready for people to board.

Baggage handling

Passengers' luggage is taken by conveyor belt from the check-in desk to the baggage handling area. As it passes through an x-ray machine, security staff watch a monitor showing detailed images of the contents of each bag.

Security staff are trained to look for suspicious items which could endanger the plane and its passengers. In particular, they look for weapons and explosives. If they are suspicious of an item of luggage, it is moved to one side for closer examination.

Luggage can only be opened in front of its owner. The barcode label attached at the check-in desk identifies which passenger the bag belongs to, and they are called over the public address system. In the meantime, security staff and customs officers may take a closer look. They use dogs trained to sniff out explosives or drugs, or a security officer may rub his hands over the bag while wearing gloves. The gloves are then analyzed for traces of dangerous or illegal substances which could be inside the bag.

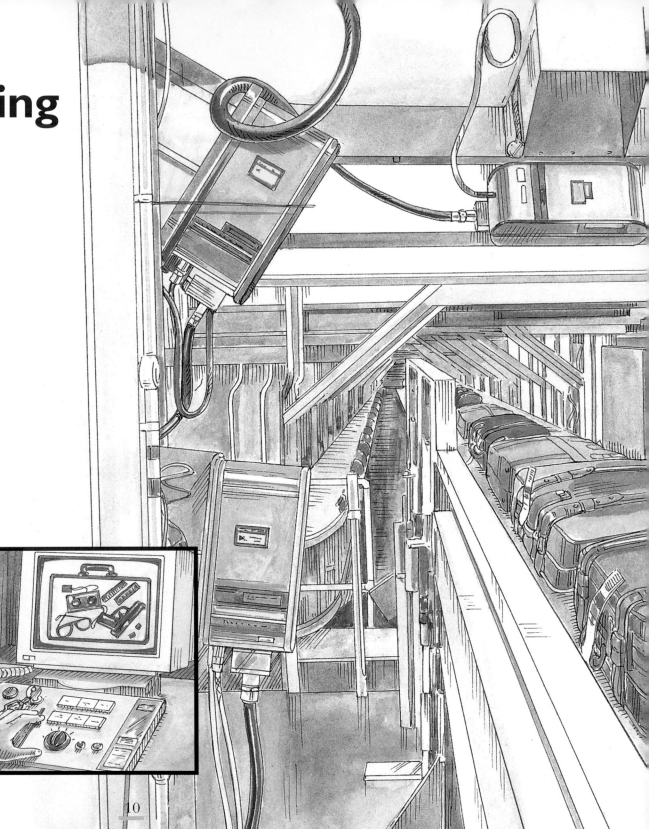

▶ X-ray machines allow security staff to see inside every piece of checked-in luggage.

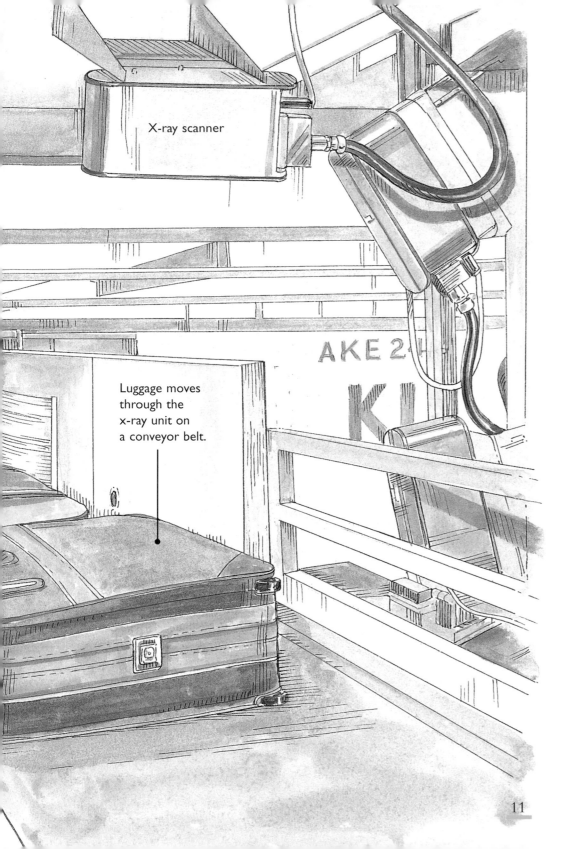

X-ray scanner

Luggage moves
through the
x-ray unit on
a conveyor belt.

AKE 2

K

▶ Sniffer dogs can smell
the faintest trace of drugs
or explosives that may be
hidden in a bag.

After the luggage has been checked and
found safe, it is sorted, ready to be loaded on
to the planes. At some airports this process is
fully automated. Scanners read each label and
a computer directs the bags down chutes to
a transporter truck. At other airports, baggage
handlers check the label on each bag by hand.
Thousands of cases pass through the baggage
handling area every day.

Baggage is spread evenly around the cargo
hold of the plane. Most planes are loaded so
they are slightly heavier at the tail end, which
makes them easier to fly.

When a plane lands at the airport, bags
and cases are unloaded and brought into the
baggage handling area, where they are placed
on a revolving conveyor belt called a carousel.
This carries the bags into the baggage claim
area, where they are collected by their owners.

On the apron

When a plane lands, it travels slowly along a taxiway towards the pier. The concrete area around the pier and the terminal buildings is the apron. Everything that goes on here is supervized by controllers in the apron control tower.

When a plane lands, controllers in the tower tell marshallers on the ground which gate to direct it to. At some airports planes are marshalled electronically to their gates. Light signals are flashed from the gate, telling the pilot exactly where to move the plane. Different types of plane have doors in positions, so each has its own place to park at the gate. For example, a Boeing 737 parks on a different spot from a Boeing 747.

When the pilot has turned off the engines, the marshaller moves a jetway into place. This is a movable corridor that connects the plane door to the gate. A computer makes sure there is a perfect link between the plane and the jetway. Passengers leave the plane, and head for the baggage claim area to collect their bags and cases.

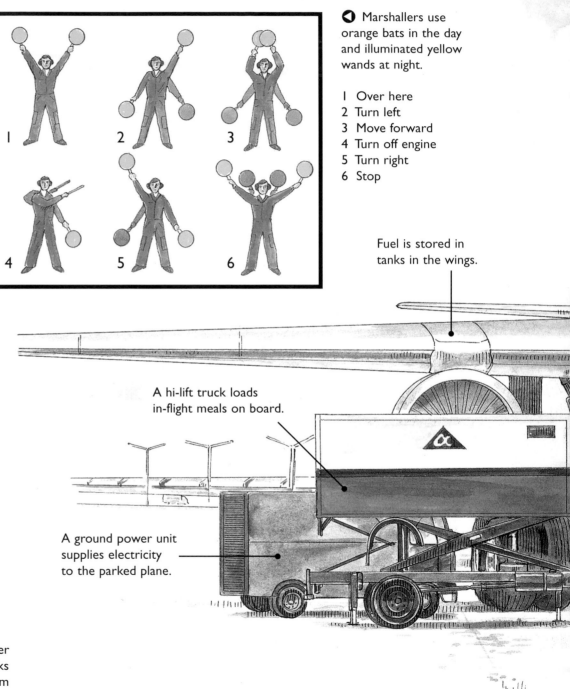

◀ Marshallers use orange bats in the day and illuminated yellow wands at night.

1 Over here
2 Turn left
3 Move forward
4 Turn off engine
5 Turn right
6 Stop

Fuel is stored in tanks in the wings.

A hi-lift truck loads in-flight meals on board.

A ground power unit supplies electricity to the parked plane.

◀ A refuelling tanker refills the plane's tanks with aviation fuel from the fuel area.

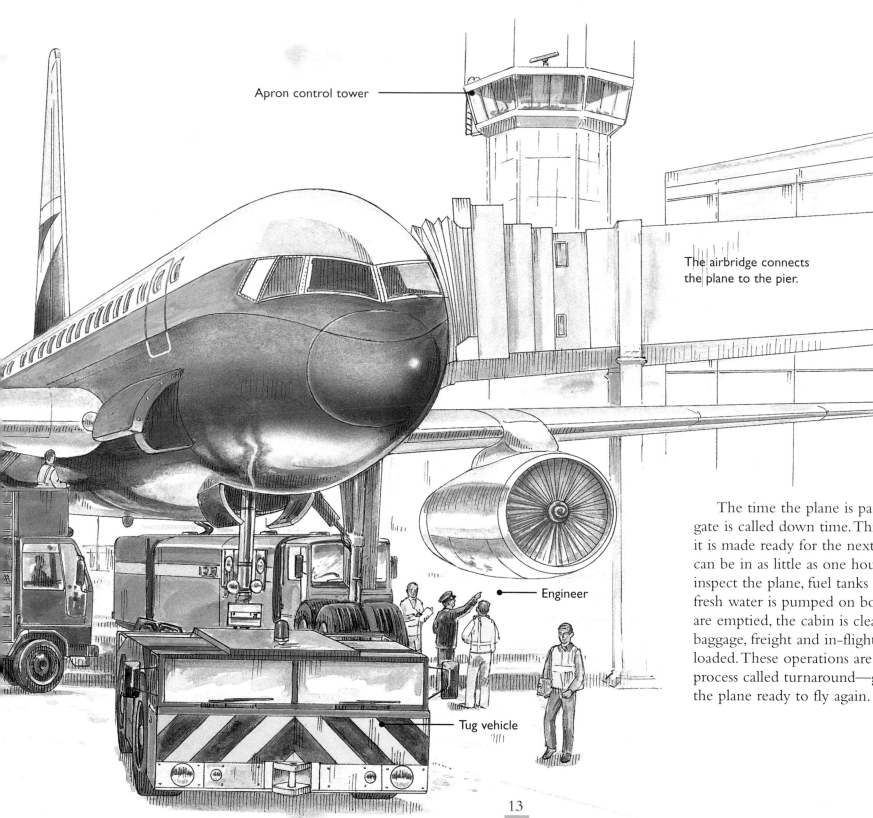

Apron control tower

The airbridge connects the plane to the pier.

Engineer

Tug vehicle

The time the plane is parked at the gate is called down time. This is when it is made ready for the next flight, which can be in as little as one hour. Engineers inspect the plane, fuel tanks are refilled, fresh water is pumped on board, toilets are emptied, the cabin is cleaned, and baggage, freight and in-flight meals are loaded. These operations are part of a process called turnaround—getting the plane ready to fly again.

Ready for take-off

About one hour before the plane is due to leave, the captain and the first officer arrive at the airport. They are the flight crew. On some planes the crew includes a flight engineer too.

Before boarding, the flight crew discuss their route and the expected weather conditions. The captain then writes a detailed flight plan. The plane cannot leave until the plan has been checked and approved by air traffic control.

In-flight meals are prepared by a catering company at the airport. They create special meals for people with particular dietary needs—such as vegetarians and diabetics, or people who do not eat certain foods because of their religion, such as Jews or Muslims. Meal trolleys are stored in a chilling room, and then taken to the holding area to be loaded on board along with cups, drinks, and newspapers.

The cabin crew—the flight attendants who look after passengers on the flight—go on board with the flight crew. Passengers follow soon afterwards. The jetway is moved back to the gate, and the plane is pushed back from the gate by a tug. The pilot turns on the engines and the plane sets off under its own power towards the runway.

Before take-off, the flight attendants tell the passengers about safety. They point out the emergency exits and lights, and demonstrate how to use the seat belts, life jackets and oxygen masks. The flight attendants then go to their own seats and the plane sets off down the runway.

△ An in-flight meal. The caterer follows strict guidelines about how each meal should be set out on the tray.

▽ A flight attendant shows how to fasten and inflate a life jacket.

14

Jetway

This dish, called a transponder, picks up radar signals from the airport.

Inside the cockpit, the captain sits on the left and the first officer on the right. On some planes a flight engineer sits behind them.

Flight attendants welcome passengers on board the plane and direct them to their seats.

Air traffic control

Planes landing and taking off are monitored by air traffic control. Air traffic controllers prevent accidents, both in the air and on the ground. They work in the control tower—a tall building with windows all around it, through which they have a good view of the airfield.

Radar scanners search for aircraft by sending pulses of sound into the sky. Planes carry a device called a transponder, which picks up the pulse and sends back a reply. The plane then shows up on the computer screens in the tower. Controllers are able to tell the direction, altitude and speed of the plane.

At a major airport the area supervized by air traffic control extends for hundreds of miles—and for thousands of yards into the air. Between airports this huge parcel of airspace is divided into lanes or airways. Each airway is a corridor about 3½ miles wide, and between 1500 and 13,000 yards high.

Controllers speak to a plane's flight crew through a headset.

▶ An air traffic controller's monitor. Each "blip" is an aircraft flying through the airport's controlled airspace.

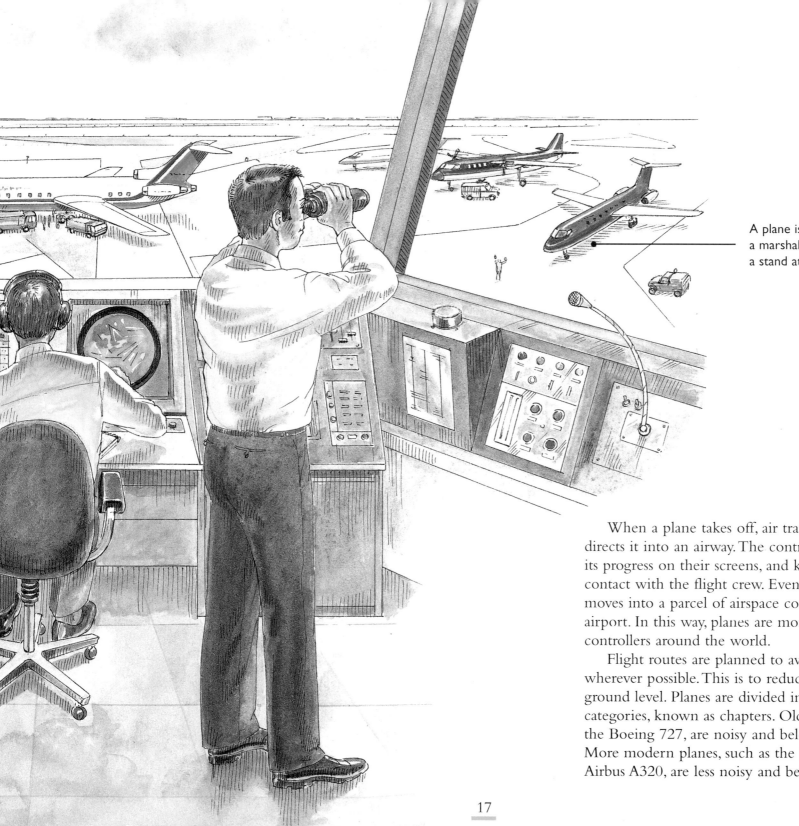

A plane is directed by a marshaller towards a stand at the pier.

When a plane takes off, air traffic control directs it into an airway. The controllers watch its progress on their screens, and keep in voice contact with the flight crew. Eventually the plane moves into a parcel of airspace controlled by another airport. In this way, planes are monitored by air traffic controllers around the world.

Flight routes are planned to avoid towns and cities wherever possible. This is to reduce noise pollution at ground level. Planes are divided into different noise categories, known as chapters. Older planes, such as the Boeing 727, are noisy and belong to chapter 2. More modern planes, such as the Boeing 757 and Airbus A320, are less noisy and belong to chapter 3.

Freight terminal

Thousands of tons of cargo and mail pass through the airport each year. Freight is brought to the airport by truck or train, and is stored at the freight terminal. This is sometimes called a cargo area.

The terminal is a busy, noisy place, open 24 hours a day. Most freight is not transported by special plane—it can be carried in the holds of passenger planes, along with passengers' luggage.

In the same way that baggage is scanned by x-ray machines, air freight is carefully checked to make sure it is safe to carry on board. Some goods, especially military items, need special permission to leave the country, and customs officers have to check that everything is in order.

All freight coming into the country is checked by customs too. They look for anything dangerous or illega—such as weapons, explosives and drugs—that could be smuggled in. They also keep a close watch on the movement of animals through the terminal. The trade in endangered species is a serious threat to wildlife. Customs officers work closely with environmental groups to stamp it out.

A hi-lift vehicle raises cargo containers up to the plane's hold.

⊙ There are heavy penalties for anyone caught trying to smuggle ivory, coral and rare animals and plants.

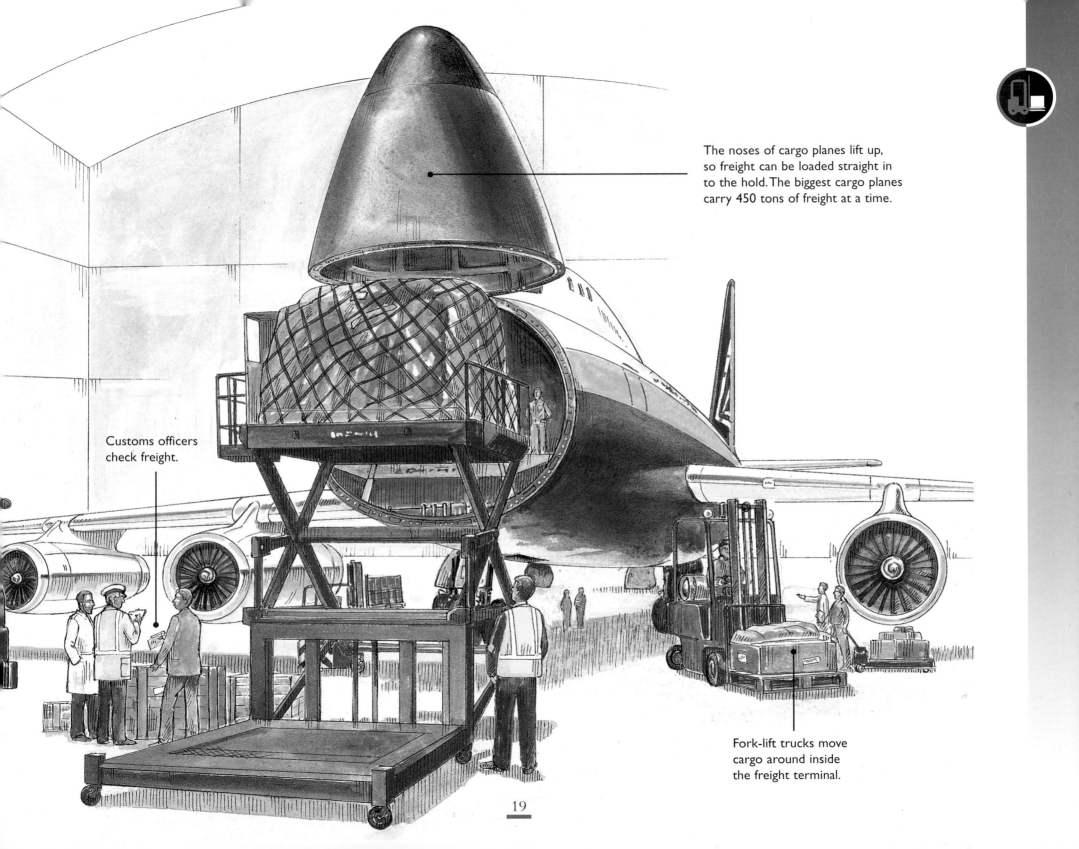

The noses of cargo planes lift up, so freight can be loaded straight in to the hold. The biggest cargo planes carry 450 tons of freight at a time.

Customs officers check freight.

Fork-lift trucks move cargo around inside the freight terminal.

Maintenance

Every time a plane lands at the airport, engineers carry out an on-the-spot safety check during down time. The plane is only allowed to fly again if it passes the inspection.

The inspection is carried out while the plane is parked at the gate. The captain and engineers discuss if there were any problems during the flight. For example, the plane might have been struck by lightning. In this case the engineers check the airframe, or body, for signs of damage, and make sure that the electronic and electrical systems are working correctly.

Tire pressures and engine oil levels are measured, wiring is examined and catches on engine covers are tested to make sure they fasten tightly. Exterior lights are switched on and off, and the engine blades are checked for damage.

◀ An engineer uses a microfilm reader to look up a diagram from the plane's service manual. The manuals contain thousands of pages of detailed instructions, so it is much easier to store them on a roll of microfilm than in a thick book.

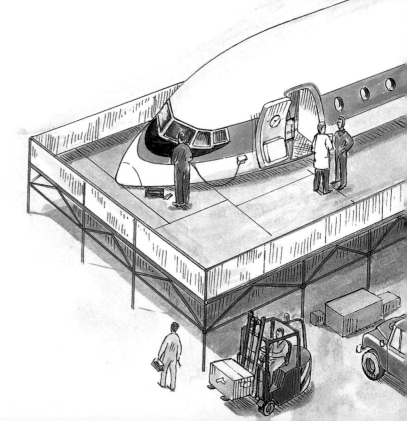

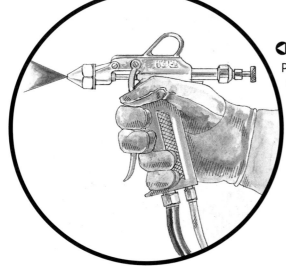

◀ When an airplane needs painting, five layers of paint are applied to the body of the plane using a spray gun. Each layer has to be completely dry before the next layer is put on.

A platform is built around the plane for engineers and painters to work on.

Once the engineers are satisfied that no repairs are needed, then the plane is safe to fly. If it is not, it goes to a maintenance hangar on the edge of the airfield.

The hangar is a huge building, big enough to hold several planes at a time. Some are simply given a routine service check, which all planes must have after a certain number of flying hours. Others may be stripped down and completely rebuilt with new parts.

The paintshop is a separate part of the hangar, closed off from the engineering areas. Here, planes are painted in the latest colors of their airline.

Emergency services

The airport has its own firefighting and ambulance services. They are on duty 24 hours a day, and are equipped to deal with all kinds of emergencies, both on the airfield and in the terminal building.

Airport firefighters aim to reach any point on the airfield in less than 90 seconds. They use special fire tenders to fight aircraft fires. The tenders smother the flames with thousands of gallons of foam or water, or a mixture of both.

Airport tenders are much larger than the fire engines used in towns. Their bodies are raised high off the ground, so that they can drive over the bumpy ground between runways without getting stuck. Large, ridged tires make sure that the vehicles do not skid at the scene of a fuel spill.

Firefighting platform attached to an extendable ladder

Equipment is stored in side lockers.

When a plane makes an emergency landing, plastic chutes unroll from the doors and fill up with air. Passengers are evacuated down the chutes as quickly as possible. Even the biggest planes can be evacuated in a few minutes.

An old aircraft fuselage is used to train firefighters.

On the edge of the airfield is an old aircraft fuselage. Firefighters use it to test their equipment and to practice handling a real emergency.

Airline crews are trained in fighting cabin fires. They also learn how to check the thousands of fire extinguishers, smoke alarms and water hydrants in the airport.

The airport's ambulance service has to deal with a wide variety of situations. If a passenger becomes seriously ill during a flight, the captain asks air traffic control to have an ambulance ready as soon as the plane lands. Paramedics take the passenger from the plane to the nearest hospital.

Around the airfield

People work at the airport night and day, not only in the terminal building, but around the airfield too. Their work is vital to the smooth running of the airport.

Bird control unit

Every airport has a full-time bird control unit. Flocks of birds can be sucked into a plane's engines, causing great damage. A control unit vehicle patrols the airfield, playing aggressive bird-of-prey calls through a loudspeaker. These are designed to scare flocks of birds away from the airfield.

Fuel area

Aviation fuel is stored in the fuel area, inside large round tanks. Fuel is delivered to planes in two ways: by tanker, or through underground pipes to refuelling points on the apron. For safety reasons, the fuel area is far away from the built-up parts of the airport.

Weather station

Weather conditions are constantly monitored around the airport. The station measures wind speed and direction, temperature, cloud cover, visibility, air pressure and humidity. Air traffic control passes the readings to approaching planes. Pilots need advance warning of storms, low cloud, fog, snow, ice and crosswinds. These conditions slow down the rate at which planes land and take off, and cause congestion in the sky.

▶ Loudspeakers on the bird control vehicle broadcast bird-of-prey calls. The driver can also fire a loud thunderflash pistol to scare rabbits and birds away from the airfield.

Plows push snow off
the airfield and runways.

▶ Each bright runway bulb
costs $350, and takes about one
minute to change. A runway can
have as many as 1500 bulbs.

Runway maintenance
Runway lights are
designed to be seen
from up to five miles
away. They are left on
all the time and last for
thousands of hours. Every
light is checked once a day.
Sometimes a pilot alerts air
traffic control that a bulb has
gone out. The maintenance team
can replace it in a few minutes.
In bad weather the team is responsible for
keeping the airport runways clear at all times.
They use plows when there has been a heavy
snowfall. If the snow is too deep to be cleared,
the airport may have to close for a time.

Airport history

1903
American pioneer Orville Wright makes the first flight in a powered aircraft at Kitty Hawk in the U.S.A. The landing strip is a field with a hut to store tools.

1910
The U.S. warship *Birmingham* becomes the first aircraft carrier, when a plane takes off from its deck.

1919
Scheduled passenger and cargo flights begin between Paris and London.

1919
The U.K.'s first town airport opens at Hounslow, outside London. Tucson Airport, in Arizona, is the U.S.A.'s first town airport.

1920s
Airports are built in and around many major European cities. Commercial air routes spread across Europe.

1929
Passenger flights start between Britain and India, with a journey time of eight days. Most of the airports along the route are just a flat desert landing strip with a hut.

Early 1930s
Regular passenger flights across the U.S.A. begin, during daylight hours only.

1932
In the U.S.A., light beacons and radio communication allow passenger and cargo planes to fly at night for the first time.

Late 1930s
The first commercial services between Europe and the U.S.A. begin, with flying boats using harbors for take-off and landing.

1976
Concorde, the first supersonic jet airliner, starts regular flights. Journey times between Europe and the rest of the world are reduced.

1950s
Runways become longer and stronger to cope with the first passenger-carrying jet planes. Airports in cities are enlarged or move to rural areas.

1970
The Boeing 747 Jumbo Jet is introduced, carrying up to 500 passengers. The growth in international air travel forces major airports to expand and modernize.

1960s
Security measures (such as metal detectors) are introduced in airports to combat the growing threat of international terrorism.

1998
Chek Lap Kok Airport opens in Hong Kong, China, on a man-made island almost 3½ miles long (see page 29). By the year 2040 the airport will handle around 87 million passengers every year.

1963
Idlewild Airport in New York, is renamed John F. Kennedy Airport in memory of the assassinated president.

1987
London City Airport opens in the Docklands area, for quiet passenger planes (called short take-off and landing jets) that use short runways.

Changing airports

The airport described in this book is a modern international airport, located close to a big city. Planes arrive and depart 24 hours a day, every day of the year, transporting people and goods around the globe. It is part of a worldwide network of similar airports, many of which began in the early part of the 20th century as small airstrips.

Aviation history was made in 1903, when Orville Wright, watched by his brother Wilbur, made the first powered flight in a heavier-than-air machine. Their plane, called *Flyer*, flew at 30 miles per hour for 12 seconds above Kitty Hawk beach in North Carolina, U.S.A.

That flight encouraged other pioneers to build their own machines. The first aerodromes, or small airports, followed soon after. The first recognizable airports, with terminal buildings and paved runways, appeared in the 1920s. Today the busiest airport in the world, Chicago's O'Hare airport, handles an amazing 70 million passengers every year!

○ U.S. navy aircraft carrier *John F. Kennedy* is a military airport at sea. Jet fighters and helicopters are carried in the ship's hold. The carrier's deck acts as the runway.

Military airports

Military planes have their own airports. These are high-security bases that are off limits to the public. The planes that use them are jet fighters and cargo planes. Many of the buildings are similar to those found at civilian airports. There are terminals, hangars and control towers, but also buildings for military staff to live in. Unlike civilian airports, military airfields are built far away from towns and cities, because much of what goes on there is secret.

◁ This photograph from 1903 shows the Wright brothers' *Flyer*, the world's first true airplane, and the basic landing strip at Kitty Hawk.

△ An aid agency relief plane lands at a basic airstrip in Somalia, Africa.

Aid airports

When a disaster, such as flood or famine, devastates a remote area, emergency supplies are needed quickly. International aid organizations, such as the Red Cross, set up airstrips to fly in food and medicine. These temporary airports are very basic, with just a landing strip and a hangar to store supplies, but they play a vital role in saving lives.

The 21st century

What will airports of the future be like? They will certainly be bigger, with larger terminals to cope with the greater volume of passengers and cargo flying around the world. Longer runways will be needed to handle the larger and faster planes of the future, such as the Airbus A3XX. This new jetliner will hold as many as 950 passengers.

Computers will take on more and more tasks at airports. One day we may fly in pilotless planes guided by a computerized air traffic control system. And perhaps the 21st century will see the development of spaceports, where passengers can board a spaceplane to the Moon or Mars just as easily as we fly to London, Sydney and New York today.

▽ Chek Lap Kok Airport opened in Hong Kong, China, in 1998. Hong Kong is so crowded that the builders had to create an artificial island to make space for the airport. The runways are built out over the sea.

Chicago O'Hare, USA - 70,385,073	
Hartsfield Atlanta International, USA - 68,205,769	
Dallas/Fort Worth International, USA - 60,488,713	
Los Angeles International, USA - 60,142,588	
London Heathrow, UK - 58,142,836	
Tokyo Haneda, Japan - 49,302,268	
San Francisco, USA - 40,493,959	
Frankfurt, Germany - 40,262,691	
Seoul, South Korea - 36,757,716	
Paris CDG, France - 35,293,378	

◁ The world's ten busiest airports, showing the number of domestic and international passengers handled in 1998.

Glossary

air traffic control The team responsible for making sure planes are a safe distance apart in the air and on the ground.

airdrome Early airports were called airdromes. The word is still used to describe small airports for private planes.

airframe The body of a plane.

airside The part of the airport beyond the security area. Only authorized members of staff and passengers with boarding cards are allowed airside.

airspace The huge parcel of air supervized by air traffic control.

airstrip A piece of land, often a field, that has been cleared so that planes can take off and land.

airway A wide lane or corridor of air about 3½ miles wide.

apron The concrete area around a terminal where planes are parked during refueling and loading.

baggage claim area The area where passengers collect their luggage after landing.

boarding pass A card given to passengers at check-in. It shows their flight details and seat number, and allows them to go to the gate and board a plane.

cabin The part of the plane where passengers sit during a flight.

cabin crew The flight attendants who look after passengers during a flight.

carousel A conveyor belt that moves luggage round in a loop in the baggage claim area.

carry-on baggage Small pieces of luggage that a passenger can take into the cabin of a plane.

chapter Planes are given a chapter number to show how noisy they are.

check-in Passengers report here when they arrive at the airport. They hand over their suitcases to be weighed, and are given a boarding pass.

cockpit The front part of a plane, where the flight crew sit. It is also called the flight deck.

control tower The controlers in this tower direct planes between the runway and the gate.

crosswind A strong wind that can push a plane off course when landing and taking off. Wind speeds are constantly monitored by the weather station.

customs A government department that checks that drugs, weapons or animals are not brought into the country illegally.

departure gate The area where passengers gather just before boarding a plane. Often it is simply called a gate.

dolly A trailer used to carry luggage around an airfield.

domestic terminal A building for passengers on flights within the same country.

down time The time a plane spends on the ground at an airport.

excess baggage charge The fee a passenger must pay if a single item of their luggage weighs more than 45 pounds.

flight crew The captain and first officer who fly the plane. Sometimes there is a flight engineer, too.

flying boat A plane that can take off and land on water. It is also known as a sea plane.

freight terminal A hangar where freight is sorted and stored until the next available flight. It is sometimes called a cargo area.

fuel area A building where aviation fuel is stored until it is pumped into a plane's gas tank.

fuselage The main body of a plane, containing the flight deck, cabin and hold.

ground power unit A vehicle that supplies electricity to a plane when it is parked at the gate with its engines turned off.

hangar A large building where a plane is taken for repairs and servicing.

headset A pair of headphones with a microphone attached, used by air traffic controllers.

hi-lift truck A truck that lifts freight up to the cargo hold of a plane.

hold The part of the plane beneath the cabin, where luggage and cargo are stored.

humidity The amount of water, or moisture, in the air.

International Phonetic Alphabet Air traffic controllers use a phonetic alphabet:

A	Alpha	N	November
B	Bravo	O	Oscar
C	Charlie	P	Papa
D	Delta	Q	Quebec
E	Echo	R	Romeo
F	Foxtrot	S	Sierra
G	Golf	T	Tango
H	Hotel	U	Uniform
I	India	V	Victor
J	Juliet	W	Whiskey
K	Kilo	X	X-ray
L	Lima	Y	Yankee
M	Mike	Z	Zulu

international terminal A building for passengers on flights between different countries.

jetway A movable corridor connecting the gate to a parked plane.

landside Parts of an airport where passengers and visitors can come and go as they please.

marshaller Someone who instructs pilots where to park their planes. They use brightly coloured bats during the day, and illuminated wands at night.

metal detector A machine that senses metal items on or inside a person's body. It is designed to find guns and knives, which are a threat to security.

passport A document that allows people to travel between countries.

pier A long corridor that connects the departure lounge to planes parked on the apron.

radar A system for tracking the positions of every plane in an airport's airspace. Pulses of sound are sent out from a transmitter at the airport and are reflected back from any planes that they hit.

runway The long strip of asphalt used by planes to land and take off.

stand The part of the apron where a plane parks.

supersonic plane A plane that can fly faster than the speed of sound, such as Concorde.

tanker A large truck that carries aviation fuel to a plane.

taxiway The concrete strip that connects the apron to the runway.

terminal An airport building for handling passengers and cargo.

transponder A tracking device fitted to all planes. When it receives a radar pulse from an airport, it sends back a reply to air traffic control.

tug A vehicle used to push and pull a plane around the apron.

turnaround The time it takes to make a plane ready for take-off.

ULD (unit loading device) Another name for a dolly.

x-ray machine A machine used to check that nothing dangerous or illegal is hidden inside luggage.

Index

Published in the United States in 1999 by
Peter Bedrick Books
A division of NTC/Contemporary Publishing Group, Inc.
4255 West Touhy Avenue
Lincolnwood (Chicago), Illinois 60646-1975, U.S.A.

Copyright © Belitha Press Limited 1999
Text copyright © John Malam 1999

Airport cutaway illustrations: David Cuzik
All other illustrations: Robin Carter
Series editor: Mary-Jane Wilkins
Editor: Russell Mclean
Series designer: Guy Callaby
Designer: Jamie Asher
Picture researcher: Diana Morris
Consultant: Ayyub Malik
Series concept: Christine Hatt

If you would like to comment on this book,
write to the author at johnmalam@aol.com

The author and publishers wish to thank Birmingham
International Airport Ltd for assisting with the development
of this book.

Library of Congress Cataloging-in-Publication Data
Malam, John.
    Airport / John Malam.
        p.   cm. — (Building works)
    Includes index.
    Summary: Reveals the inner workings of a typical modern
airport, exploring the airfield, other key places, and what takes
place there.
    ISBN 0-87226-586-2
    1. Airports Juvenile literature.   [1. Airports.]   I. Title.
II. Series.
TL725.M35   1999
387.7'36—dc21   99-14504
                                                             CIP

Printed and Bound in China

International Standard Book Number: 0-87226-586-2

99 00 01 02 03 15 14 13 12 11 10 9 8 7 6 5 4 3 2 1

Picture acknowledgements:
Dennis Gilbert/View: 29br. Clive Newton/MPL: 28tr.
TRH: 28bl, /USAF: 29tl.